To the pugs.

little ☕ *cup*

ISBN 978-1-950003-01-3
First Printing, 2021
Printed in the United States of America

Fine more Inkpugs at:
www.inkpug.com

Contents

TASTY:

a Second Helping of Pug Poetry by *inkpug*

Pugs at Home

It growled! It prowled!
It roared its roar!
Now, thanks to me,
it roars no more.

You're welcome.

The morning migration of Liz
iz a trek from spot to spot:
To where the sun iz riz,
from where the sun iz not.

Dino-pug, the Pug-o-saurus,
rules the prehistoric forest,
stamping,
tramping
over swamps
in tiny
little
puggy
stomps.

Kip would be Instagram famous!
His pathway to fame would be steep!
　　Yes, he'd be on top
　　just as soon as mom stopped
posting pics of him, halfway asleep.

: clik :

Squirt grew up with squirrels!
The squirrels taught Squirt all!
    If treats were hid
    atop the fridge,
old Squirt would climb the wall!

Georgiana the library pug
curled up with her fav'rite books, snug.
    When ushered away
    at the end of the day,
she smuggled some out in her chub.

I gave the backyard
a perimeter search;
I growled at the pigeons
all smug on their perch.
I chewed up a toy,
I rolled in your bed,
I listened to none
of those "no's" that you said.
I barked at the neighbor,
I pooped on the rug . . .

I could've done more,
but I'm only one pug.

Chelle can't see your hiding spot,
for sight is something she has not.
But she can hear the slightest squeak:
That's how she wins at hide & seek.

Old Pickleball loved
when his dad tossed him up:
as weightless and spry
as he'd felt as a pup.

Glo
likes
baths,
but
only
when
she
brings
her
bacon
bath-soap
in.

Pug not in right now:
gone on secret pug bizness.
Send dinner through flap.

And now:
Bucky Ding-Dong,
and the Dance
of a Thousand Doorbells!

Pugs
at Work

He has an "I hate Mondays" mug!
He's got some jaunty ties!
Now, can he please go to work,
and not be left behind?

Big Boule was a famous food critic;
At restaurants, Big Boule dined for free.
    He'd swagger inside,
    take a table for five,
and order up dinner for three.

Jinji was an astronaut!
His rocketship carried him far.
　　He floated in space
　　with a spherical grace:
A planet, amidst all those stars.

For all of your fancy events,
please hire these musical gents!
They'll play the top ten,
an encore, and then,
they'll eat up their own instruments!

Vilma and Velma McPeasy
were the first pugs to run a speakeasy.
 They didn't serve drinks,
 despite what you'd think,
just people food, served extra-cheesy.

Jepson paints paintings
so bold and so bright;
Her artistic touches
are always just right!
When asked for her secrets
she won't divulge much,
except for this tip:

"It's all in the brush!"

She whips, she whirls,
she twists, she twirls!
Her tail, like a flag unfurls!
Of all the rinks
in all the world,
there's only one pug roller girl!

Jake hangs out at truck stops.
He likes the way it feels
when other truckers gather 'round,
admiring his wheels.

Sarsparilla joined the opera!
Sarsparilla's doing great!
They've yet to make the glass
that Sarsparilla cannot break!

Need a message sent with care?
Buddy Boy will get it there!
He may not be the speediest,
but he puts the 'pee' in U-P-S.

Shrek had a job at Chez Pita,
as a customer greeta and seata.
At the end of his shift,
as a small parting gift,
they gave him a pita to eata.

Around the old shipyards,
you're like to hear gab
'bout old Cap'n Curly,
once clinched by a crab.

Each sailor who tells it
adds one to the line
of the creatures what pinched
Cap'n Curly's behind.

Food

First we eat breakfast,
and then we eat lunch,
and then we eat more . . .
'cause that ain't enough.

"Doc, oh Doc! What have I got, and how shall I endure it?"
"It's sausage-itis, my dear boy, but I know how to cure it!"
grumble
grumble

Marta's fav'rite muffins
include apple, corn and bran.
A reach for Marta's muffins
is a risk to your whole hand.

Ribbet makes floats!
He scoops 'em himself!
To hold Ribbet's floats
takes a mighty strong shelf!

This is the face
that's letting you know:
I should have been fed
thirty seconds ago.

Oh, hi . . . did u call?
I heard crinkling through the wall,
and a breeze
of fresh cheese
drew me near.

I see that ur eatin' . . .
I hope u'll be treatin'
ur favorite lil' pug
who's RIGHT HERE.

Brad had his own way
of thanking the chef:
the better the meal,
the deeper the stretch.

She dreamt she had
her own drumstick,
but woke before
she got a lick.

Maybe
Icarus

should
have
attempted
his
flight

after
pizza
night

What do you put in pug stew?
A turkey! A pizza! A shoe!
Now stir it (or not)
in a pan (or a pot),
then break out a bowl and a spoon!

Annabelle thought she might try
to bake a from-scratch pumpkin pie.
   She gave it a shot,
   but, pie, it was not,
and she couldn't quite figure out why.

The rain kept on falling,
and Reg was not thrilled . . .
though it helped that his water
stayed freshly refilled.

When Hildy slept
upon her food,
she woke up in
a better mood.

Pug-sistential Thoughts

Got a pug question?
Gaps in your knowledge?
Facts you ain't learnt
in your time at Pug College?

Fear not! Just consult
this new Pug-cyclopedia:
a thrilling collection
of pug-centric media!

You may not see words,
but just take a whiff:
the entire thing's written
in plain scratch & sniff!

What is the best way
to share a warm bed?
With one at the foot,
and one at the head.

Soft is the fur,
and wet is the nose,
and warm is the bottom
that sits on your toes.

Pug perseverance
cannot be ignored.
After four dinners,
they'll beg you, "Four more!"

Little Miss Clover
is both neat and rude.
She licks her paws clean
when she steps in your food.

Roses are red.
They come in a bunch.
If you really love me,
you'll give me your lunch.

Melvin looked upon his treat;
His treat seemed very small.
When he was wee,
treats used to be
much *bigger*, he recalled.

Lana was banned from the deli
for stealing a steak and a chop.
    Lana would never
    try sneaking back in
in a silly disguise like this box.

Joey the Gardener
will water your beds . . .
For a dollar, he'll water
your neighbors', instead.

Pease combines
her yawn and sneeze
for maximum
efficiency!

Tiff eats chowder undisturbed
on visits to the dock.
She always flies
a box of fries
as payment to the flock.

Someone is gone.
I wait here?
I move on?
A minute?
A day?

It's okay?

It's okay?

The
LOOK

Wherever she went,
her nickname was Bat.
Why'd everybody
keep CALLING her that?

All Prim's hats were wrong for brunch!
None had the perfect trim,
    'til her haberdasher
    put a rasher
of bacon on the brim.

Allie was a pugicorn!
No-one could tell her no!
There was no rule
(not that she knew)
'bout WHERE the horn should go!

There was an old fancy named Claire,
who wore flowers pinned up in her hair!
    With many a rose
    overhanging her nose
she won big at the Pug County Fair!

Jim forgot his towel,
so he used the groomer's spare.
    The problem was,
    the towel, 'twas,
at best, just partly there.

Sometimes, in dreams,
Sherelle felt a glimmer
of her previous life
as a synchronized swimmer.

As Gimli brushed and brushed and brushed,
a worry made him frown:
Was there a pug at the bottom of this?
Was he fur,
all
the
way
down?

My word . . .
they ARE marvelous,
aren't they?
No wonder everybody's always asking for 'em.

Pug & Friends

Donut-hole-in-one!
Truly, we need accomplish
nothing more today.

Stinky McSparkles Jerome GI Joe
was named by four children
who each loved him so.
All were his fav'rite,
and none he'd forego;
thus, Stinky McSparkles Jerome GI Joe.

There once was a pug on a sail,
whose boat got turned 'round in a gale.
  "Oh, help me!" cried he,
    to the gods of the sea,
and was promptly towed home by a whale.

Hugsy McGee was the friendliest pug!
A friendlier pug, there was none!
   She was friendly enough
   to charm most of the world . . .
though a little *too* friendly for some.

Dolores
was never
afraid of the dark,
after
she met
a new friend in the park.

With pork pie hat
and stylish spats,
Dickey tried
to wow the cats.

I rolled the snow
into a lump;
I drawed a tail
upon the rump;
I gived him eyes
so he could see;
I maked a friend
to play with me!

Yes, thought Vanderbilt,
this could be the start of a
beautiful fir-endship.

More Food

There was nothing to lose
(and SO MUCH to gain)
if Beefsteak Tomatoes
lived up to their name.

Persephone's donuts were PERFECT.
Her recipe worked rather nicely:
    five ounces of donut,
    two ounces of frosting,
and ninety-six sprinkles precisely.

Fudge is a famous orator!
It's agreed (among all those who rate her)
    that no one speaks nearly
    as wisely or clearly
as Fudge, munching
french-fried potaters.

She heard it loud,
she heard it clear:
The ice cream truck
was drawing near!

"Come outside,"
its chimes rang, sweet,
"The ice cream man
will give you treats!"

From a deep, deep sleep,
Marcella awakened.
Did she hear bacon
being baconed?

Sizzle
Sizzle

Fred never stole snackies,
not even when tempted!
Unless it was pizza...
then Freddy relented.

A few more beans
and she'd make the grade
as the newest pug float
in the Macy's parade!

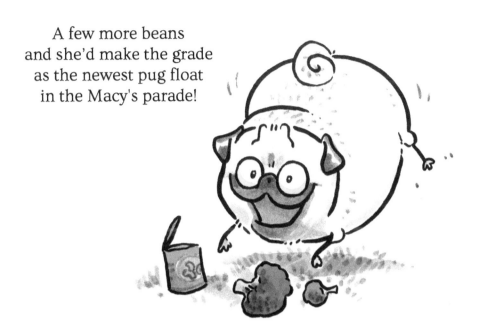

Three square meals a day
had taken their toll!
It was time to go back
to her little round bowl!

Geraldine Grooby
makes magical things:
cupcakes that sing,
and knishes with wings!

Her creations, though grand,
rarely last until dinner,
and Geraldine Grooby
is getting no thinner.

Did I buttter this side?
Can't remember;
better butter.
Did I butter that side?
Can't remember;
better butter.
Did I butter this side?
Can't remember;
better butter.
Did I butter that side?
Can't remember;
better butter.
Did I butter this side?
Can't remember;
better butter.
Did I butter that side?
Can't remember;
better butter . . .

Garth was a choosy old fellow,
who, though blind, liked his cheese to be yellow.
    Everybody knew better,
    than to give Garth white cheddar:
He'd know it was white by the smell-o.

Ballou went to college with all of his plates
(and his spoons, and his knives, and his forkses).
    At his first lecture hall,
    he stormed out, appalled:

I've completely misunderstood COURSES!

Zito worked at Pizza Plus.
At night, he slept in dough:
    all cozy in
    his pizza skin . . .
a little pug calzone.

Freeze pops, freeze pops,
those bite-the-top-and-squeeze pops,
those sure-do-beckon-bees pops,
those whole-box-just-for-me pops . . .

Wait, lemon lime?
Ugh, never mind.

Whenever someone orders Tony's,
Emmy smells like pepperonis.

Out West, there lived a cowpug pup,
and once a year, he saddled up,
to make a long and dusty ride:
the Conestoga Meatball Drive.

He drove those meatballs 'cross the plains,
through whistling winds and sleeting rains,
over canyons, rills, and ridges,
to Mama Rosa's waiting fridges.

And when his cowpug work was done,
the Meatball Kid had lost just one:
Ev'ry meatball, hand-delivered...
'cept the one he ate for dinner.

au natural

The leaves took flight . . .

as did Emmy,
with her kite.

When the weather is wet
and the squishy mud sloshes,
pug soccer is played
in one's finest galoshes!

Mary has a special spot;
That spot is white with snow.
The snow had better melt real quick,
'cause Mary's got to *go*.

I move to make the rain illegal!
I vote to ban the clouds!
I need to live where wet is not
a thing that is allowed!

Fresh black coffee,
a hot egg-and-cheese,
and a paper to read,
in the park, under trees.

Peg waits 'til the blossoms
come up to her nose,
then pretends she's a sled dog
asleep in the snow.

If you're very polite
when you speak to their queen,
you can get ants to tickle
your tummy, FOR FREE!

Miss Everleigh let out a wail
when she chanced to encounter a snail.
"How dreadful," thought she.
"Somewhere there must be
some poor pug who is missing her tail!"

A rugged young puggy named Ross,
loved hiking, but at quite a cost.
    Along with the treezes
    came myriad sneezes:
Nature, with pollendaise sauce.

Noble buttercup,
the wisest of all flowers:
these chins tell no lies.

How does it KNOW?

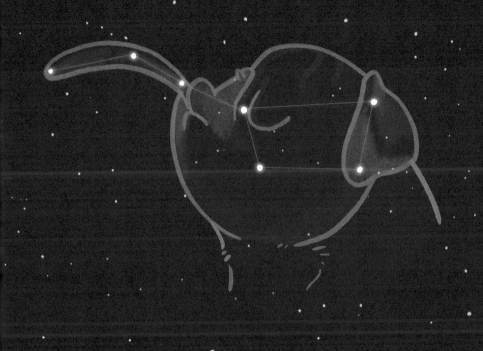

That constellation . . .
doesn't it look exactly
like a pug, tasting?

Puppies in orbit!
Puppies in space!
Eight puppy planets
are spinning with grace!
The sun makes them bright
amidst all the dark,
and comets in flight make them
bark-bark-bark-bark!

Special
Pug-casions

Her Gotcha Day comes once each year,
and Luz wakes early, just to hear
the kitchen sounds, as mama bakes
her very special Gotcha Cake!

Game Night

Pug-nopoly gets things started
and Gin Puggy is a hoot;
Pug-gammon brings a welcome break
from Trivial Pug-suit.

A little Texas Pug 'Em
and an hour of Pug-cassonne,
then Pug-tionary to wrap things up
before some Pug of Thrones!

His hot dog permit's squared away!
He'll take whatever he pleases!
Grilling season starts today,
and he doesn't do 'catch-and-releases'!

You had your fun on the Fourth of July
and now, I hope you're through . . .
The next one to set off a firework
is getting a poop in their shoe!

Rosie liked jet planes
with big sonic booms,
and rumbly old freight trains
that passed by her room.
She listened to punk rock
at maximum volume . . .

Fireworks?

Nah, they weren't a problem.

At family reunions,
Melissa kept busy
by testing which foods
she could throw like a Frisbee.

This pumpkin had come
with an oven inside . . .

if Bub waited patiently,
THERE WOULD BE PIE.

Let's decorate for Halloween!
Let's terrify the crowds!
You play the spooky music,
and I'll make some ghastly clouds.

Halloween movies,
on the TV,
you might scare the humans,
but you can't scare me!

Bert was an old pug vam-pie-re!
His cravings could not be denied!
To fulfill his dark need,
Bert stole pies to feed
on the syrupy fillings inside.

Count Dracula once had a pug
who simply refused to drink blood!
   Type O, B, or A,
    she sent all away,
and opted for steak and a hug.

Halloween dreams,
achieved. Time to make room
for Thanksgiving dreams.

Snow Day: when I do
all my usual nothings
but it feels *SPECIAL!*

Turn up the heat--
dis pug's wasting away!
You take me to park,
I too frozen to play!
I try curl my tail,
and curl will not stay!
For warmth, I need eat
18 pizzas a day!
It pizzas, or heatzas;
now, what do u say?

'Tis Christmas morn,
and Tim's on the lam,
after secretly eating
the whole Christmas ham.

Resolutions can wait.
Happy New Year!
Sleep late.

He lit his candles every day;
Each day he blew them out.
Each day would be his birthday
'til they burned the whole way down.

Booboo reads *lots* of pug poetry.
He has my first book on his shelf!
    But he felt it was rude
    that I didn't include
any poems 'bout Booboo himself.

(For Booboo. Please stop writing me.)

CPSIA information can be obtained
at www.ICGtesting.com
Printed in the USA
BVHW022139190122
626602BV00004B/244